My Little Book of
Dinosaurs

by Dougal Dixon

QEB

QEB Publishing

Editor: Ruth Symons
Designer: Punch Bowl Design
Art director: Laura Roberts-Jensen
Editorial director: Victoria Garrard

First published in the United States by
QEB Publishing, Inc.
3 Wrigley, Suite A
Irvine, CA 92618

www.qed-publishing.co.uk

A CIP record for this book is available from the
Library of Congress.

ISBN 978 1 60992 802 5

Printed in China

Words in **bold** are explained in the glossary on page 46.

Contents

What is a dinosaur?

Dinosaurs were a group of **reptiles** that lived hundreds of millions of years ago, during the **Triassic**, **Jurassic**, and **Cretaceous** periods.

˅ **Like modern reptiles, dinosaurs laid eggs.**

FACTS

Dinosaur Timeline

Cretaceous
145 to 65 million years ago

Jurassic
200 to 145 million years ago

Triassic
250 to 200 million years ago

Dinosaurs came in all shapes and sizes. Some ate meat, while others ate plants. Some walked on two feet while others walked on all fours.

∨ **Dinosaurs ruled Earth for 160 million years.**

∨ **The dinosaurs all died out about 65 million years ago.**

Archaeopteryx

(Ark-ee-op-ter-ix)

Today's birds are related to meat-eating dinosaurs. *Archaeopteryx* was the very first bird.

>> ***Archaeopteryx*** **was about the size of a modern crow, but with a long tail.**

<< ***Archaeopteryx*** **did not have a beak. Instead it had jaws and teeth like a lizard.**

Archaeopteryx had the wings and feathers of a bird, but the head, hands, and tail of a dinosaur.

⌄ *Archaeopteryx* had fingers and claws that it used for climbing trees.

FACTS

Archaeopteryx

Size
17 inches long

When it lived
Late Jurassic

What it ate
Smaller animals and insects

Microraptor

(Mike-row-rap-tor)

Microraptor was a tiny feathered dinosaur. It is the smallest dinosaur that has ever been found.

« *Microraptor*'s back legs were covered in feathers.

FACTS

Microraptor

Size
15–24 inches long

When it lived
Early Cretaceous

What it ate
Insects and fish

Microraptor had feathers on its arms, legs, and tail. It could not fly, but it was so small and light that it could **glide** from tree to tree.

« *Microraptors* glided through the forests.

9

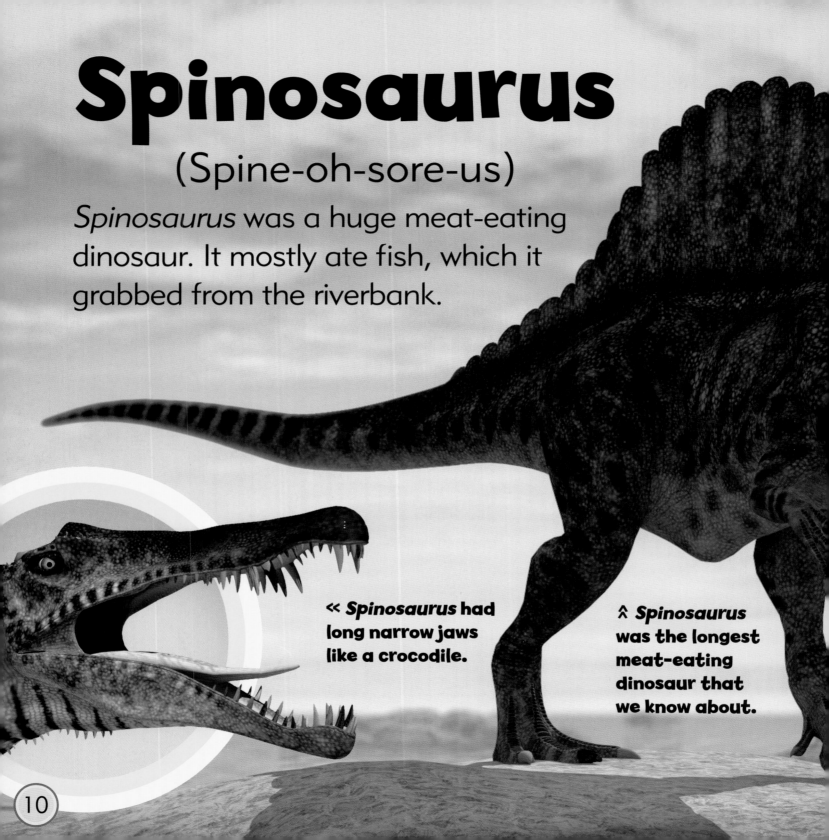

Spinosaurus

(Spine-oh-sore-us)

Spinosaurus was a huge meat-eating dinosaur. It mostly ate fish, which it grabbed from the riverbank.

« *Spinosaurus* had long narrow jaws like a crocodile.

⌃ *Spinosaurus* was the longest meat-eating dinosaur that we know about.

Spinosaurus had a huge **sail** of skin on its back. This was brightly colored so that it could show off to impress a **mate**.

⌄ *Spinosaurus* had a huge curved thumb claw. It used this to hook fish out of rivers.

FACTS

Spinosaurus
....

Size
56 feet long

When it lived
Early Cretaceous

What it ate
Fish and pterosaurs

Tyrannosaurus

(Tie-ran-oh-sore-us)

Tyrannosaurus was the biggest
meat-eating dinosaur that ever lived.

⌃ *Tyrannosaurus* had
eyes that faced
mainly forward. This
helped it to spot **prey.**

« *Tyrannosaurus* killed its prey with its huge bladelike teeth.

Tyrannosaurus walked on two strong back legs. It prowled the forests of North America hunting and eating other big dinosaurs.

FACTS

Tyrannosaurus
....

Size
40 feet long

When it lived
Late Cretaceous

What it ate
Other dinosaurs

» Despite its huge size, *Tyrannosaurus* had tiny arms.

Velociraptor

(Vel-oss-ee-rap-tor)

Velociraptor was the size of a fox and a deadly killer. It had a long, sharp claw on each back foot.

⌄ ***Velociraptor*** **hunted in packs. This meant it could hunt dinosaurs much bigger than itself.**

FACTS

Velociraptor

Size
6.5 feet long

When it lived
Late Cretaceous

What it ate
Other dinosaurs

In a fight, *Velociraptor* used its killer claws to attack prey.

>> **When *Velociraptor* walked, it lifted its claws up and away from the ground.**

Oviraptor

(Oh-vee-rap-tor)

Oviraptor was a small dinosaur with feathers and a beak. It looked a bit like a bird.

⌄ *Oviraptor* **made nests in the sand, and sat on its eggs to keep them warm.**

FACTS

Oviraptor

Size
6 feet long

When it lived
Late Cretaceous

What it ate
Eggs and small animals

Oviraptor raided the nests of other dinosaurs. It would grab eggs in its big hands and break into them with its beak.

⌃ **Oviraptor had a beak like a bird's, but with tiny teeth on the roof of its mouth.**

Diplodocus

(Dip-lod-i-kus)

Diplodocus was a long-necked plant-eating dinosaur. It was one of the longest dinosaurs ever.

FACTS

Diplodocus

Size
88 feet long

When it lived
Late Jurassic

What it ate
Low-growing plants, or leaves from the trees

⌄ *Diplodocus* lived on wide, open plains, feeding on leaves in the trees.

Diplodocus had a long, low-slung neck. It could use its tail like a whip, to scare away **predators**.

≫ *Diplodocus* could probably stand on its back legs to reach the tops of trees.

Brachiosaurus

(Brak-ee-oh-sore-us)

Brachiosaurus was one of the tallest long-necked plant-eaters. It held its head in an upright position, a bit like a giraffe.

>> **Brachiosaurus had a long neck that made up half of its height.**

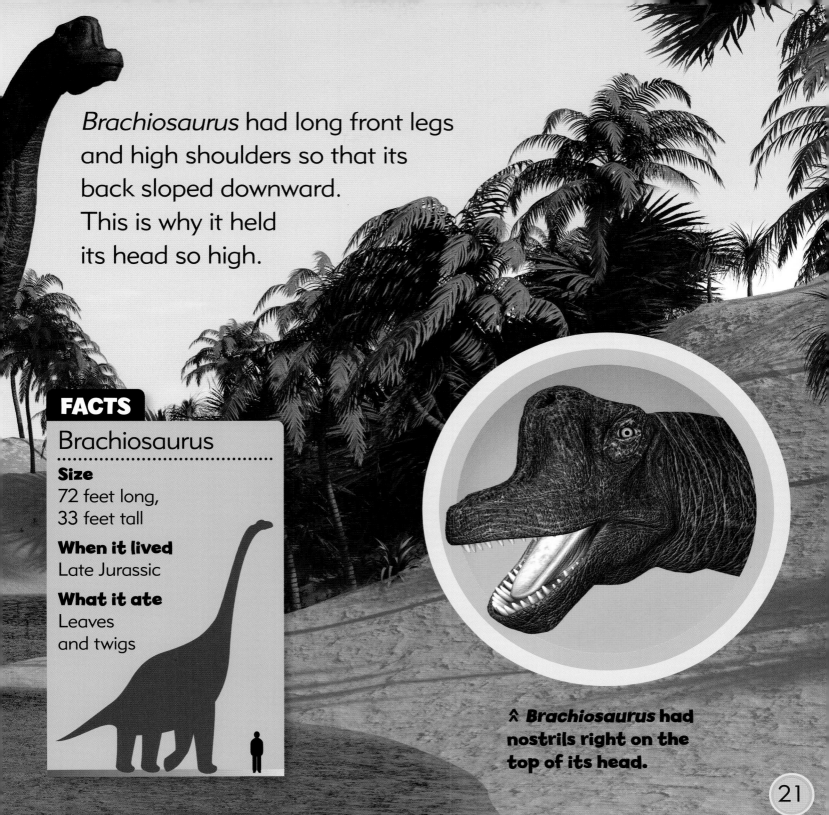

Brachiosaurus had long front legs and high shoulders so that its back sloped downward. This is why it held its head so high.

FACTS

Brachiosaurus

Size
72 feet long,
33 feet tall

When it lived
Late Jurassic

What it ate
Leaves
and twigs

⌃ *Brachiosaurus* had nostrils right on the top of its head.

Argentinosaurus

(Ahr-gen-teen-oh-sore-us)

Argentinosaurus was the biggest and heaviest dinosaur ever discovered.

⌃ *Giganotosaurus* was one of the only meat-eaters big enough to threaten *Argentinosaurus*.

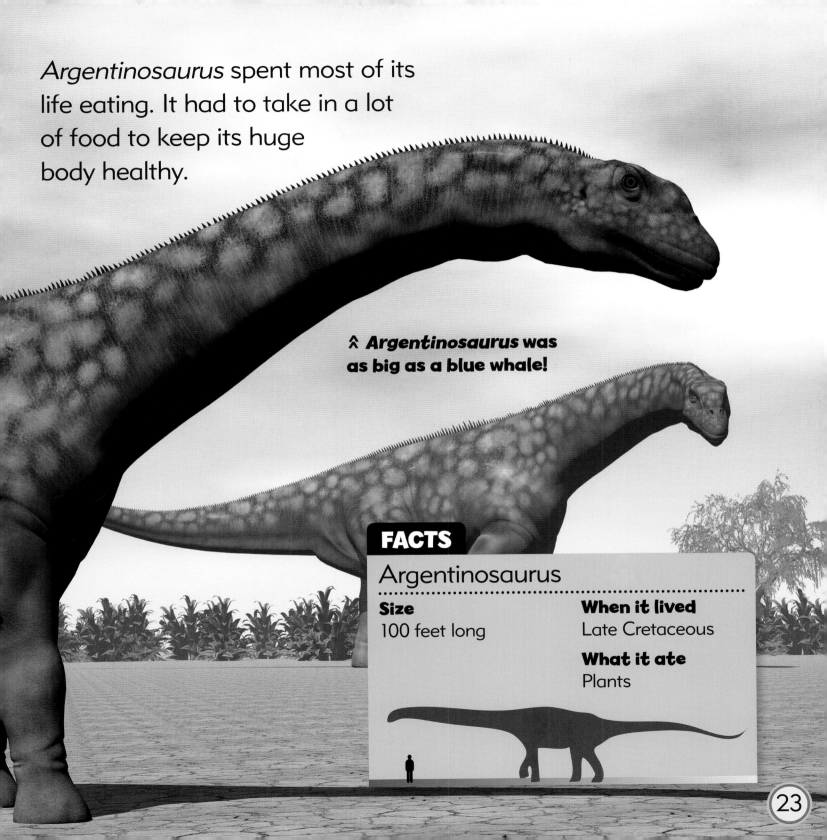

Argentinosaurus spent most of its life eating. It had to take in a lot of food to keep its huge body healthy.

⌃ **Argentinosaurus was as big as a blue whale!**

FACTS

Argentinosaurus

Size
100 feet long

When it lived
Late Cretaceous

What it ate
Plants

Iguanodon

(Ig-wan-oh-don)

Iguanodon was a large plant-eating dinosaur. It usually walked on four legs but could stand or run on two.

FACTS

Iguanodon

Size
33 feet long

When it lived
Early Cretaceous

What it ate
Plants

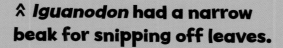
⌃ *Iguanodon* had a narrow beak for snipping off leaves.

⌄ *Iguanodon* lived in herds around **swamps**.

Iguanodon could eat low-growing plants or it could sit back on its hind legs to reach leaves in the trees.

⌄ *Iguanodon* had a sharp thumb spike for ripping down leaves or fighting off enemies.

Parasaurolophus

(Par-ah-sore-oll-oaf-us)

Parasaurolophus was a plant-eating dinosaur with a hollow **crest** that swept back from its head.

⌄ *Corythosaurus*, a relative of *Parasaurolophus*, had a crest shaped like a helmet.

« *Parasaurolophus* used its crest as a trumpet to make a loud noise!

» *Olorotitan* had a crest shaped like an ax blade.

Several dinosaur **species** had crests on their heads. They were all different shapes and colors so that dinosaurs could tell each other apart.

FACTS

Parasaurolophus

Size
33 feet long

What it ate
Plants

When it lived
Late Cretaceous

27

Stegosaurus

(Steg-oh-sore-us)

Many plant-eating dinosaurs were covered in **armor**, or had plates or **horns** to protect themselves.

FACTS

Stegosaurus

Size
30 feet long

What it ate
Plants

When it lived
Late Jurassic

✔ *Stegosaurus* had four long spikes on its tail. It could use these to fight off meat-eating dinosaurs.

Stegosaurus had a double row of plates down its back. These guarded it from attacks. They were also used for showing off to impress other dinosaurs.

>> *Kentrosaurus* was a smaller relative of *Stegosaurus*.

Ankylosaurus

(An-kie-low-sore-us)

Ankylosaurus was a large, plant-eating dinosaur, covered in bony armor.

>> **Ankylosaurus was the biggest of all the armored dinosaurs.**

⌃ *Ankylosaurus* had a huge bony club on the end of its tail.

⌃ *Ankylosaurus* even had armored eyelids.

It had armor plates on its head, neck, and tail. These were made of bone covered in horn and protected *Ankylosaurus* from predators.

FACTS

Ankylosaurus

Size
36 feet long

When it lived
Late Cretaceous

What it ate
Plants

31

Triceratops

(Try-sair-a-tops)

Triceratops was a four-footed plant-eater with a neck shield and horns on its face.

⌃ *Triceratops* had a big beak used for snipping off bits of food.

Triceratops was similar to a modern rhinoceros. It had a big body, thick legs, and horns on its face. Like a rhinoceros, it ate low-growing plants and leaves from bushes.

>> *Styracosaurus* was also a horned dinosaur. It had six long spikes around its neck shield and one on each cheek.

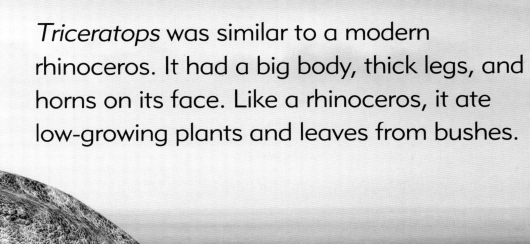

Rhamphorhynchus

(Ram-for-ink-us)

At the time of the dinosaurs, the skies were full of flying reptiles called **pterosaurs**.

∧ *Rhamphorhynchus* **had a long tail, with a flap on the end, which it used for steering.**

Rhamphorhynchus was one of the earliest pterosaurs. It had a hairy body and long, leathery wings. Each wing was supported by one enormous finger.

⌃ *Rhamphorhynchus* had sharp teeth for snatching up fish as it flew low over water.

⌃ *Rhamphorhynchus* had a body the size of a crow, but with long, narrow wings.

FACTS

Rhamphorhynchus
....

Size
5.5 feet wingspan

When it lived
Late Jurassic

What it ate
Fish and squid

Quetzalcoatlus

(Ket-zal-coe-at-lus)

As time went by, the pterosaurs became bigger and bigger. *Quetzalcoatlus* was as big as an airplane!

∧ *Quetzalcoatlus* was probably the biggest animal that ever flew.

« When it was on the ground, *Quetzalcoatlus* walked on all fours and was as tall as a giraffe.

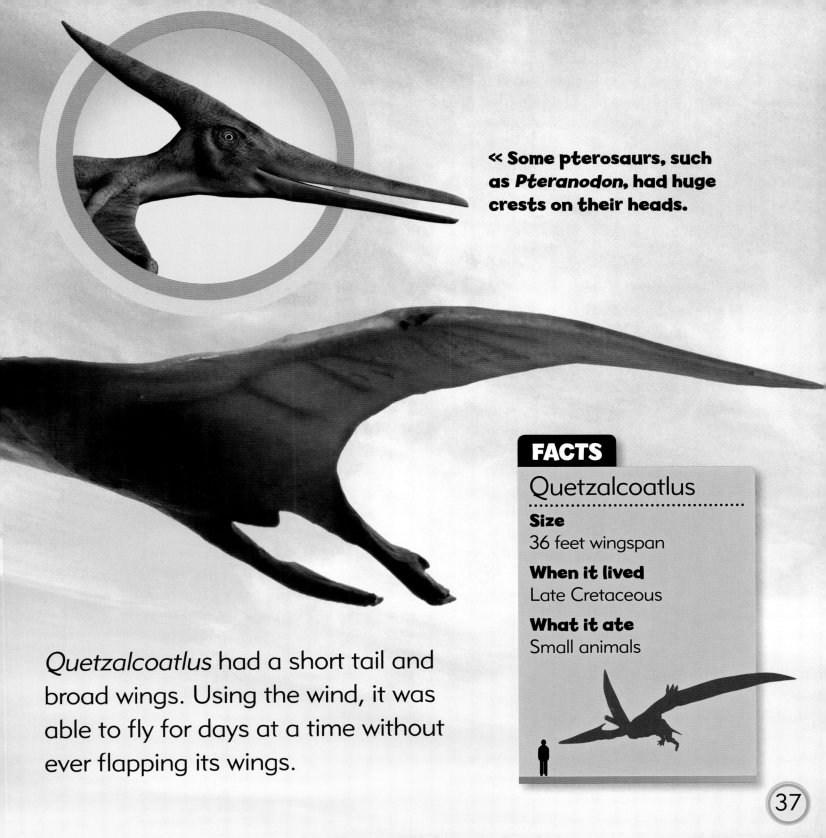

« Some pterosaurs, such as *Pteranodon*, had huge crests on their heads.

FACTS

Quetzalcoatlus

Size
36 feet wingspan

When it lived
Late Cretaceous

What it ate
Small animals

Quetzalcoatlus had a short tail and broad wings. Using the wind, it was able to fly for days at a time without ever flapping its wings.

Ichthyosaurus

(Ick-thee-oh-sore-us)

Ichthyosaurus was a small, fishlike reptile with a long, pointed **snout**.

« *Ichthyosaurus* ate fish and ammonites —animals that lived in spiral shells.

Ichthyosaurus looked and lived just like a fish. It had a streamlined shape and pointed fins on its back and tail.

⌄ The name *Ichthyosaurus* means "fish lizard."

^ *Ichthyosaurus* had huge eyes for hunting in deep, dark waters.

FACTS

Ichthyosaurus

Size
6.5 feet long

When it lived
Early Jurassic

What it ate
Fish and ammonites

Mosasaurus

(Mow-za-sore-us)

Mosasaurus was one of the biggest reptiles swimming in the oceans. It preyed on seabirds, large fish, and other sea reptiles.

<< **Mosasaurus was the terror of the seas at the end of the Cretaceous period.**

« *Mosasaurus* had such strong jaws that it could crush turtle shells.

Mosasaurus had a body shaped like a crocodile's, but with powerful flippers instead of arms and legs. It had a long snout lined with sharp teeth.

FACTS

Mosasaurus

Size
60 feet long

When it lived
Late Cretaceous

What it ate
Fish, ammonites, and other swimming reptiles, such as turtles

How fossils form

We know all about dinosaurs thanks to **fossils**—pieces of dinosaur bone preserved in rocks.

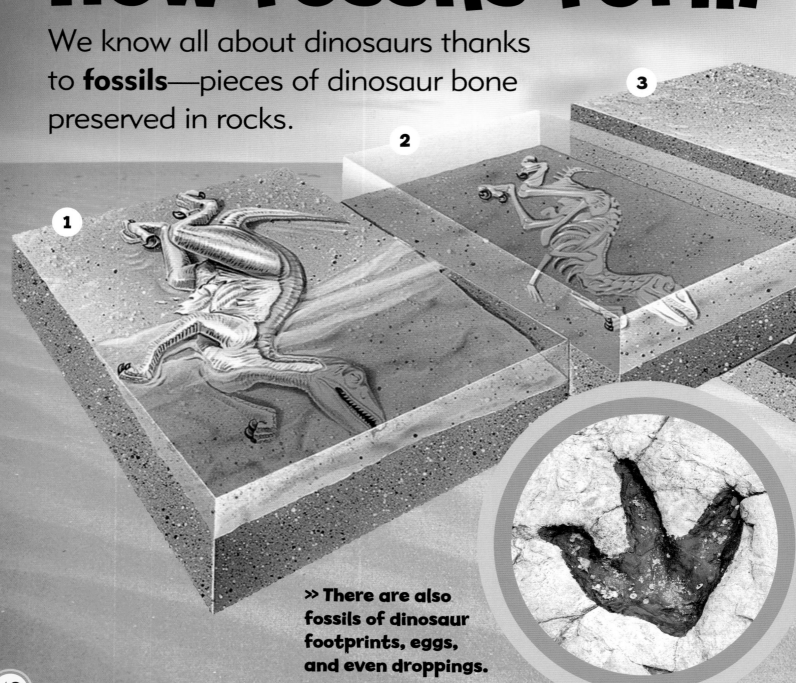

>> There are also fossils of dinosaur footprints, eggs, and even droppings.

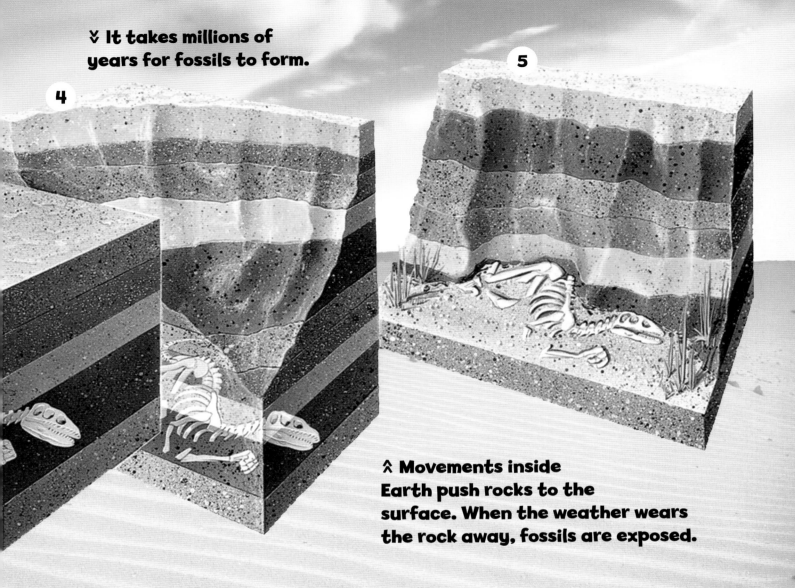

⌄ It takes millions of years for fossils to form.

4

5

⌃ Movements inside Earth push rocks to the surface. When the weather wears the rock away, fossils are exposed.

Fossils formed when a dinosaur's remains were covered quickly by mud or sand. As the mud and sand was packed down over time, it turned into rock. Inside the rock, the dinosaur's bones turned to stone.

Dinosaurs today

It takes a lot of work to get a fossil out of the ground and into a museum!

⌄ Scientists that study dinosaurs are called **paleontologists.**

⌃ This is a dinosaur skeleton mounted in a museum.

Most museums make models of fossils to use in their displays. The original fossils are kept safely behind the scenes for scientists to study.

⋎ **Scientists study fossils closely to learn how dinosaurs lived.**

Glossary

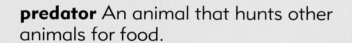

armor A protective covering.

claw A curved, pointed toenail on an animal. Some dinosaurs used their sharp claws as a weapon.

crest A bony growth on an animal's head or back.

Cretaceous The period of time between 145 and 65 million years ago. The dinosaurs suddenly died out at the end of this period.

fossil The remains of something that lived a long time ago, now turned to stone in the rock.

glide To fly without flapping.

horn A hard, pointed growth on an animal's head.

Jurassic The period of time between 200 and 145 million years ago.

mate An animal's partner for breeding.

pack A group of animals that live and hunt together.

paleontologist A scientist who studies ancient animals and plants.

predator An animal that hunts other animals for food.

prey An animal that is hunted by a predator.

pterosaur A flying reptile that lived at the time of the dinosaurs.

reptile A cold-blooded animal that usually lives on land and lays eggs.

sail A sail on a dinosaur's back was like a fin on a fish's back.

snout The nose and jaws of an animal.

species A group of animals that look like each other and can breed together.

swamp An area of land that is always wet and flooded.

Triassic The period of time between 250 and 200 million years ago. The first dinosaurs appeared at the end of the Triassic period.

Index

Picture credits

(t=top, b=bottom, l=left, r=right, c=center, fc=front cover, bc=back cover)